This Italic Handwriting notebook belongs to:

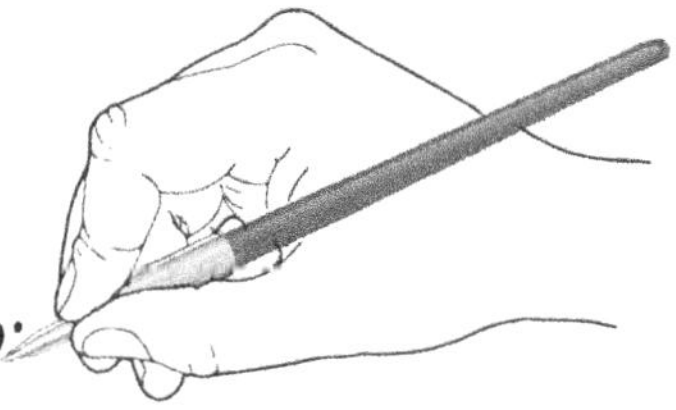

Published by

MOVE APP STUDIO, LLC

Introduction

During my senior year in high school, I was an exchange-student at Pomfret School, a boarding school for boys in Pomfret Center, Connecticut. I saw an announcement at school about an Italic Handwriting Competition based in Newport, Rhode Island. If I remember correctly, it was sponsored by the Arts Association of New England Preparatory Schools. On a lark, I decided to create an entry for the competition purely based on chutzpah and self-taught skill honed with my father's artistic tutorials.

When my art teacher Charles Cole saw my entry, he volunteered to hand-deliver my creation to the competition sponsor for fear it would not arrive on time or it would be damaged in the mail. He drove with my entry from Pomfret Center all the way to Newport, Rhode Island. To my surprise, I won the competition with another entrant and received an Osmiroid calligraphic pen set which I still have to this day and $150 in prize money, which was a lot of money in those days.

This was the start of my life-long love for italic handwriting. I often use it to address personal envelopes or create fancy flyers or any personalized messages I am requested to create.

Beginners to dip pen calligraphy can start with a Basic Calligraphy Set from Speedball which is available on Amazon for around $12. More advanced users can opt for the Daveliou Calligraphy Pen Set also available on Amazon for about $45.

There are 4 basic things to remember when doing calligraphic handwriting:

1. *Hold the pen tip at a 45 degree angle.*
2. *The letters have slight forward slant.*
3. *The lower-case letters often require single strokes and infrequently require pen lifts.*
4. *The capital letters which are fancier require more strokes and pen lifts.*

The following page shows the strokes required for the capitals and lower-case characters used in Italic Handwriting. Of course, there is nothing to prevent you from using your own preferred strokes to produce the letters. The succeeding pages are all lined pages to serve as a guide to practicing your Italic Handwriting.

Have fun with your Italic Handwriting journey!

Win Villamora

Italic Alphabets

Capitals

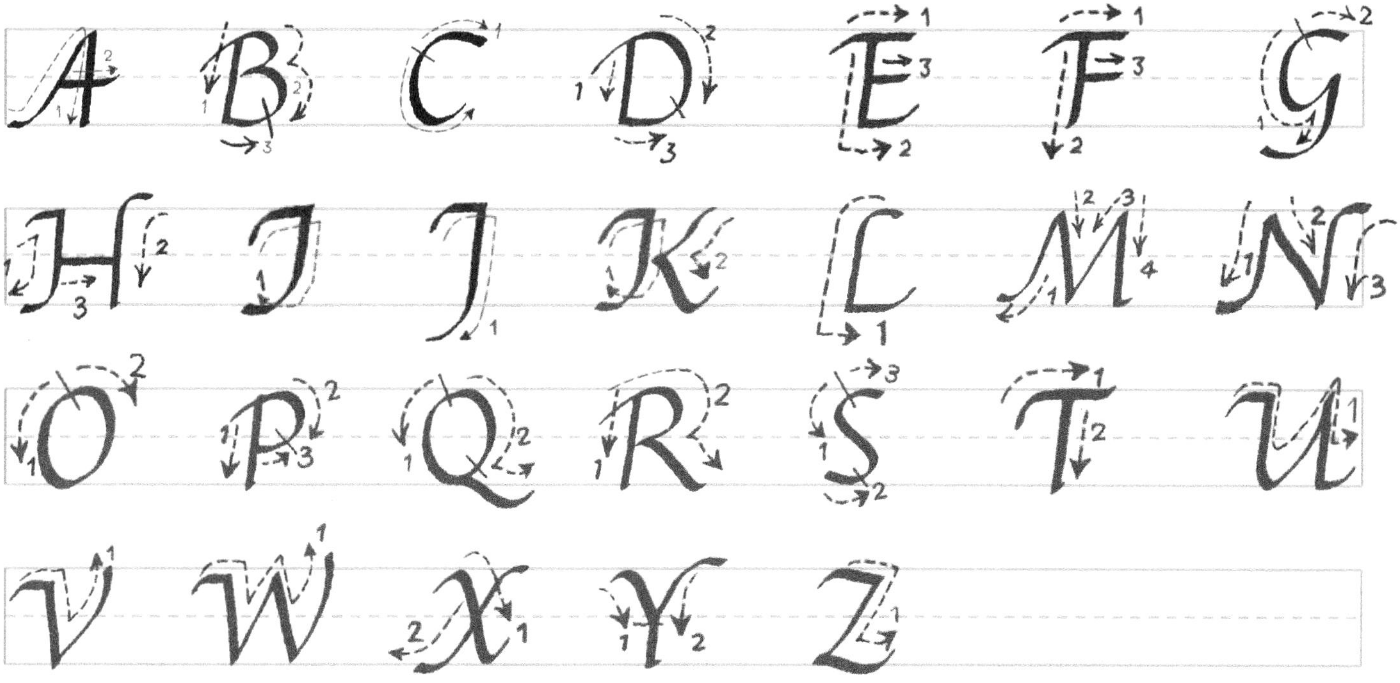

Lower-Case

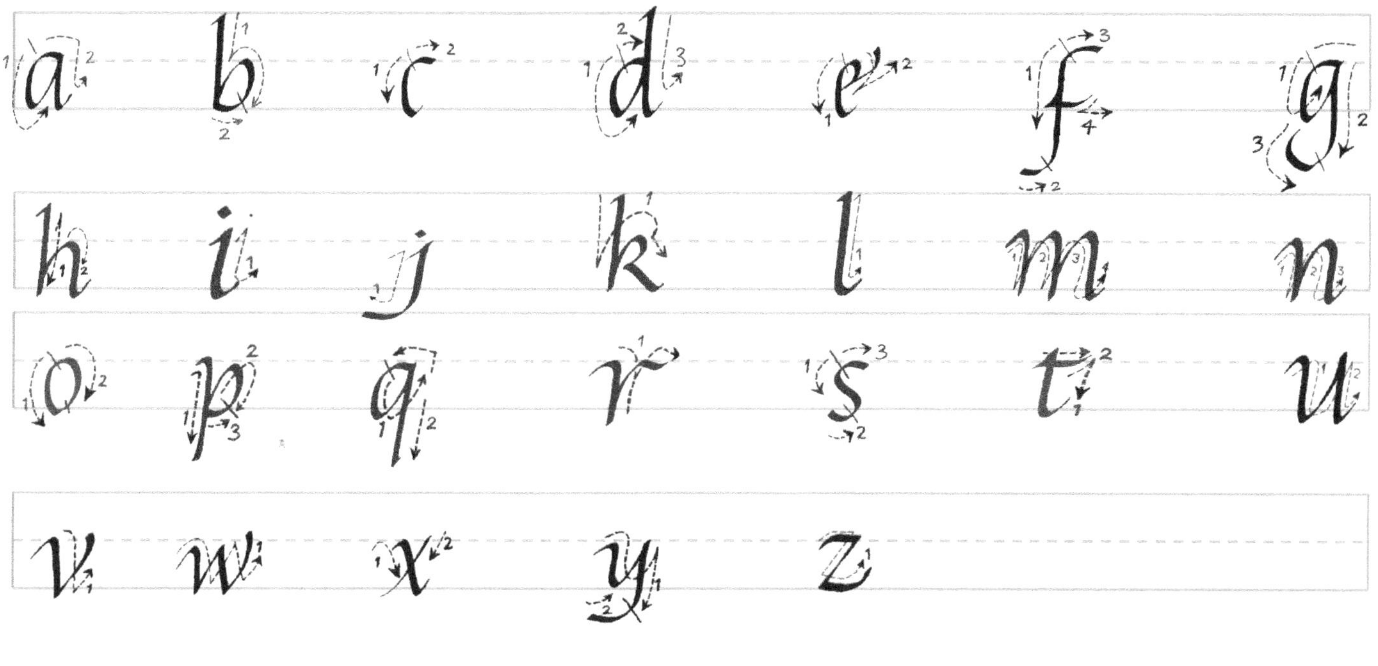

Made in the USA
Monee, IL
14 January 2024

51766697R00070